CONTENTS

Words in the glossary appear in **bold** type the first time they are used in the text.

AN IMPORTANT LIFE

Benjamin Franklin led a very eventful life. He's the only Founding Father to have signed all four **documents** that helped create the United States, including the Declaration of Independence in 1776 and the US Constitution in 1787. The others are the Treaty of Alliance with France in 1778 and Treaty of Paris with England in 1783.

But Benjamin was much more than a **diplomat**. Benjamin was a printer, an inventor, a scientist—and a great swimmer!

Did You Know?

Born in Massachusetts in 1706, Benjamin was British at birth since the colonies were still under the rule of Great Britain then.

Benjamin Franklin

Benjamin had 16 brothers and sisters, though some died before he was born. His father was a soap and candle maker who tried to ready Benjamin for a job in the **clergy** by sending him to school. Benjamin didn't go for long, though. Much of what he learned he taught himself by reading throughout his life.

Benjamin even taught himself to swim by reading a book! He made swim fins out of wood to help him paddle faster. The fins were one of his first inventions.

Benjamin's swim fins

Did You Know?

Benjamin was known as such a good swimmer that he was made an honorary member of the International Swimming Hall of Fame in 1968.

Young Benjamin did well in writing, but poorly in math, when he was in school.

7

LIFE AS AN APPRENTICE

When Benjamin was 12, his father sent him to be an **apprentice** to his brother James, a printer. While Benjamin was learning about printing, the brothers didn't always get along. It's well known that Benjamin wrote letters under the name "Silence Dogood" for his brother's newspaper without his brother knowing. But did you know James was very angry when he found out?

Later, James was thrown in jail for some views he put in the paper. Benjamin kept the paper going until his brother got back. Instead of being happy, James beat and yelled at Benjamin!

printing press

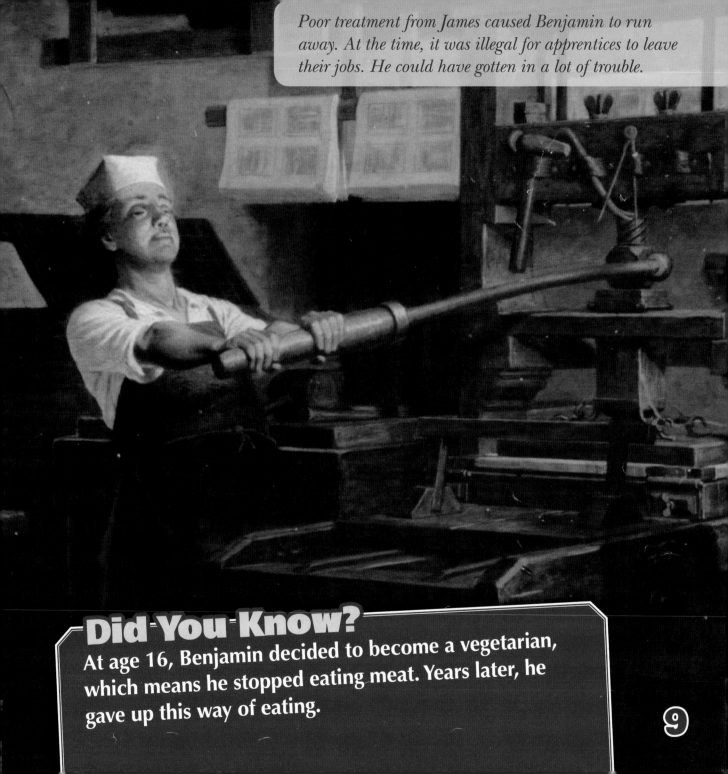

Poor treatment from James caused Benjamin to run away. At the time, it was illegal for apprentices to leave their jobs. He could have gotten in a lot of trouble.

Did You Know?

At age 16, Benjamin decided to become a vegetarian, which means he stopped eating meat. Years later, he gave up this way of eating.

Benjamin tried to find work as a printer in New York City. When that didn't work, he walked all the way across the state of New Jersey to Philadelphia, Pennsylvania! Upon arriving, he met Deborah Read, who became his wife in 1730. He also began his long career as a printer in the city.

For much of the 1730s and 1740s, Benjamin was a successful businessman. His print shop printed paper money for Pennsylvania and Delaware. At the same time, he and Deborah ran two other stores!

Colonial money

front   back

Did You Know?

Benjamin not only established a library, **volunteer** fire company, and hospital in Philadelphia, but he also established one of the first **insurance** companies!

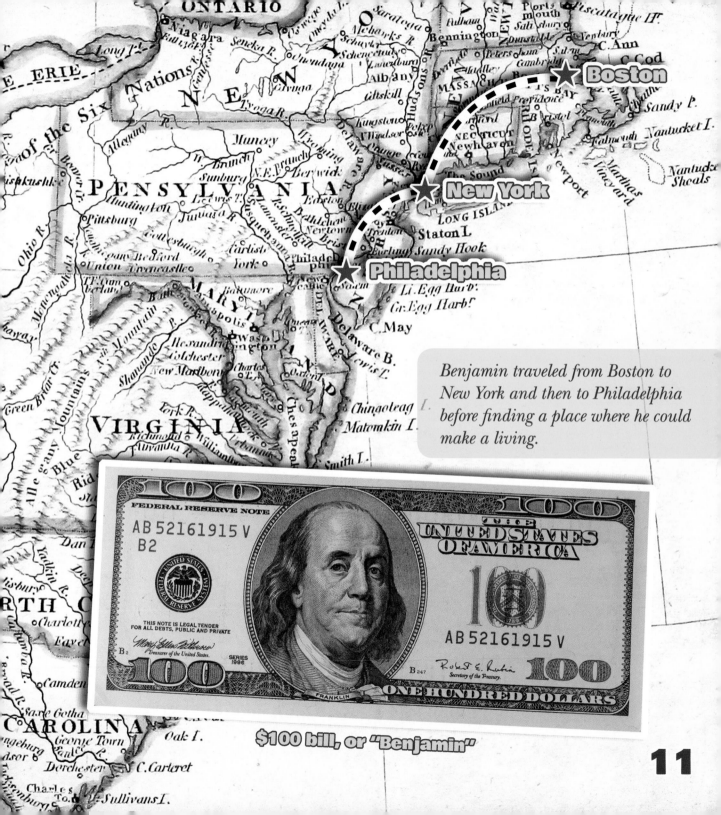

Boston

New York

Philadelphia

Benjamin traveled from Boston to New York and then to Philadelphia before finding a place where he could make a living.

$100 bill, or "Benjamin"

POOR RICHARD AND FRIENDS

"Silence Dogood" was a pseudonym (SOO-duh-nihm), or pen name, Benjamin used. "Richard Saunders" was another famous pseudonym of Benjamin's. Known as "Poor Richard," Saunders was the character Benjamin used to write his *Poor Richard's Almanack*, the source of many of his most famous phrases.

But Benjamin wrote under several other pen names! Many of these, such as "Alice Addertongue" and "Anthony Afterwit," "wrote" columns in the *Pennsylvania Gazette*. Benjamin used the name "Benevolence" to write corrections in British papers when they included negative ideas about Americans.

Did You Know?

Benjamin bought a newspaper called the *Pennsylvania Gazette* in 1729. In it, he drew and published the first **political cartoon**.

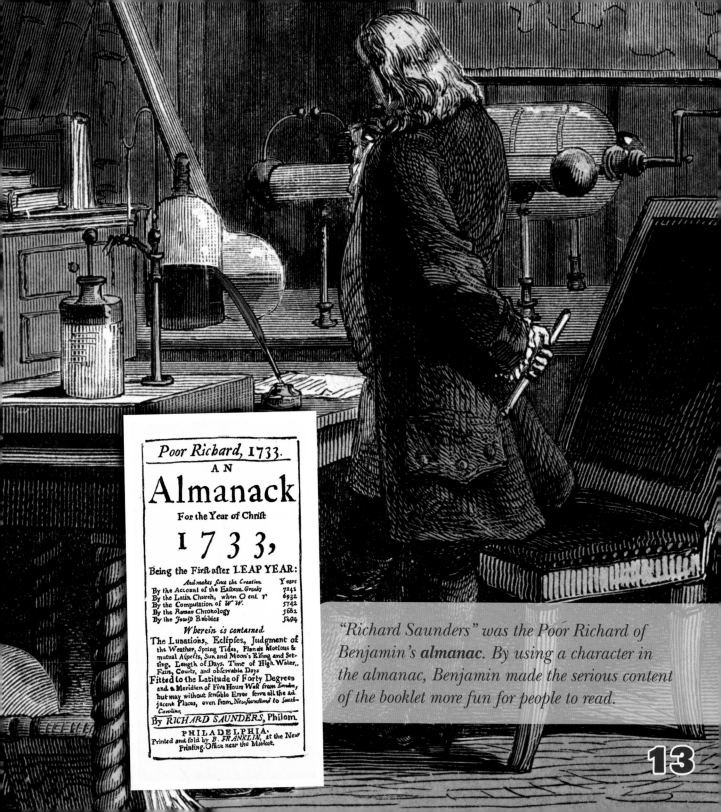

"*Richard Saunders*" *was the Poor Richard of Benjamin's* **almanac**. *By using a character in the almanac, Benjamin made the serious content of the booklet more fun for people to read.*

13

THE INVENTOR AND SCIENTIST

You may know that Benjamin invented the Benjamin stove, bifocals, and the lightning rod. But during his life, especially after he retired from his printing business around 1749, he invented many more items! Some of these include the **odometer** and an "arm" that could be used to reach high shelves.

Benjamin also studied science and weather. He observed the properties of lightning and charted the **Gulf Stream**. Some of the first weather **forecasts** are recorded in *Poor Richard's Almanack*!

Did You Know?

In addition to inventing an instrument called the glass harmonica, Benjamin wrote music and played the violin, harp, and guitar.

Benjamin's experiments with electricity began during the 1750s. They were dangerous. Twice, Benjamin was knocked out by electric charges!

15

Benjamin was concerned with doing good for those around him. He wouldn't file for a **patent** on many of his inventions because he only wanted them to benefit others. He started printing cartoons and pictures in his almanac and newspaper so those who didn't read could understand the daily happenings.

From 1757 to 1775, Benjamin **represented** Pennsylvania in England. Like many others, Benjamin became interested in American independence during this time. His wife died while he was gone.

Did You Know?

Benjamin's son William became the royal governor of New Jersey. William was against American independence. This caused a lasting division between him and Benjamin.

Benjamin, along with John Adams (center) and Thomas Jefferson (right), took part in the writing of the Declaration of Independence.

When Benjamin was sent to France in 1776, he was already 70 years old. His job was to convince the French government to support the American Revolution. Benjamin was successful, even though he didn't speak French very well!

Benjamin was so popular in France, his face was put on watches and rings. Women styled their hair to look like a fur hat he wore. In 1780, at the age of 74, Benjamin asked a French woman named Madame Helvetius to marry him. She said no.

Did You Know?

John Adams went to France to help Benjamin and other diplomats make peace with England. Adams and Benjamin didn't get along at all!

Benjamin's fur hat

By the time Benjamin went to France, he was already well known in Europe for his scientific studies. It would be the seventh time he crossed the Atlantic Ocean in his life!

19

AT THE END

In 1783, Benjamin asked Congress to bring him home from France. His request wasn't granted until 2 years later. He was already 79, but that didn't stop Benjamin from taking part in writing the new nation's constitution. It wasn't always a serious task to him. Stories say that Benjamin used to trip people walking by his seat on the aisle!

When Benjamin died in 1790, about 20,000 people attended his funeral. Even then, Benjamin was known as a Founding Father and a true American.

Did You Know?

Just a few of the buildings and places named for Benjamin Franklin include the Benjamin Franklin Bridge connecting Philadelphia and Camden, New Jersey; a submarine called the USS *Benjamin Franklin*; and Franklin, Pennsylvania.

Quotable Benjamin

Many phrases still used today come from this Founding Father's life and writing:

A penny saved is a penny earned.

Early to bed and early to rise, makes a man healthy, wealthy, and wise.

An ounce of prevention is worth a pound of cure.

Remember that time is money.

By failing to prepare, you are preparing to fail.

GLOSSARY

almanac: a book with a calendar and facts such as the moon's cycles, sunrises and sunsets, and the weather expected in a given year

apprentice: someone who learns a trade by working with a skilled person of that trade

clergy: a leader in religious services

diplomat: a person who is skilled at talks between nations

document: a formal piece of writing

forecast: an informed guess about future weather

Gulf Stream: the warm current in the Atlantic Ocean that comes from the Gulf of Mexico and moves along the US coast

insurance: an agreement in which a person pays a company for a guarantee of money in case of damage, illness, or death

odometer: a tool that measures distance

patent: a document that gives an inventor the only rights to make, use, or sell their invention for a certain time

political cartoon: illustration drawn to suggest a message about current events or people

represent: to stand for

volunteer: to work without pay

FOR MORE INFORMATION

Books

Crawford, Laura. *Benjamin Franklin from A to Z*. Gretna, LA: Pelican Publishing, 2013.

Freedman, Russell. *Becoming Ben Franklin: How a Candle-maker's Son Helped Light the Flame of Liberty*. New York, NY: Holiday House, 2013.

Websites

Benjamin Franklin FAQ
learn.fi.edu/franklin/birthday/faq.html
Find the answers to many questions about Benjamin Franklin's life.

Liberty's Kids Archive: Benjamin Franklin
www.libertyskids.com/arch_who_bfranklin.html
Learn more about Benjamin Franklin's inventions and life.

INDEX